Ipswich

TROLLEYBUSES

Colin Barker

Series editor Robert J Harley

MP Middleton Press

Cover Picture: Karrier 112 turns out of Clapgate Lane ready for the return to town as it passes under the crossover for wiring that continues along Landseer Road (Authors collection).

> *For almost 40 years trolleybuses, many built locally by Ransomes, Simms & Jefferies and Garrett, plied the streets of Ipswich with the system having been one of the first all tram to trolleybus conversions in the United Kingdom. This publication provides a cameo of those years that will be remembered by older generations and will illustrate to others a form of electrically powered pollution free public transport that had rapid, smooth and virtually silent acceleration.*

Published June 2005

ISBN 1 904474 59 4

© *Middleton Press, 2005*

Design Deborah Esher

Published by
> Middleton Press
> Easebourne Lane
> Midhurst, West Sussex
> GU29 9AZ

Tel: 01730 813169
Fax: 01730 812601
Email: info@middletonpress.co.uk
www.middletonpress.co.uk

Printed & bound by Biddles Ltd, Kings Lynn

CONTENTS

INTRODUCTION & ACKNOWLEDGMENTS

Although Derby is my hometown I have lived in Suffolk since 1991 when I moved to the area with my employment and the interest in trolleybuses stems from childhood exposure to the Derby, Nottingham and Hastings systems in the 1940s. My only experience of the Ipswich system was during a works trip to Stowmarket and Felixstowe whilst I was an apprentice in the mid 1950s with the only sighting of a trolleybus being a long distance view of the Priory Heath depot forecourt.

Having completed a book on the trolleybuses of my hometown, the editor suggested that a similar book on my adopted local town of Ipswich would keep me occupied during my retirement.

There have been many changes to the centre of Ipswich since the trolleybus era of 1923-1963. To obtain a flavour of the period it has been necessary to consult the many "Ipswich past" books published over the years and refer to contemporary Ordnance Survey maps and commercial postcards.

This book is not a definitive history of the system but more a photographic journey that takes the reader along the roads of this county town which was served by trolleybuses for virtually 40 years. Whilst the contents will interest those who study public transport it should bring back nostalgic memories to those who travelled the system on a regular basis.

The arrangement of photographs follows each main route out from the two central termini, namely Cornhill and Electric House (now Tower Ramparts) and I have endeavoured to minimise views seen in other publications.

The photographs chosen originate from a variety of sources with many taken by individual enthusiasts. Where the photographer and the source are known due accreditation has been given but some views give no indication to their originators. I hope they accept that their work has been included to enhance this publication for a wider audience.

Thanks go to the Ipswich Transport Museum, sited in the old Priory Heath trolleybus depot, for use of photographs from their collections and to John Gillham for the use of his comprehensive route map. Not being a native of Ipswich I have had to rely heavily on local enthusiasts who have readily answered my continual questions and points of detail and in particular Brian Dyes, Bob Markham and John Langford of Ipswich plus Stan Letts of West Midlands; the first three made numerous constructive suggestions on reading through the first draft. Thanks again go to my wife Maureen for her word processing skills.

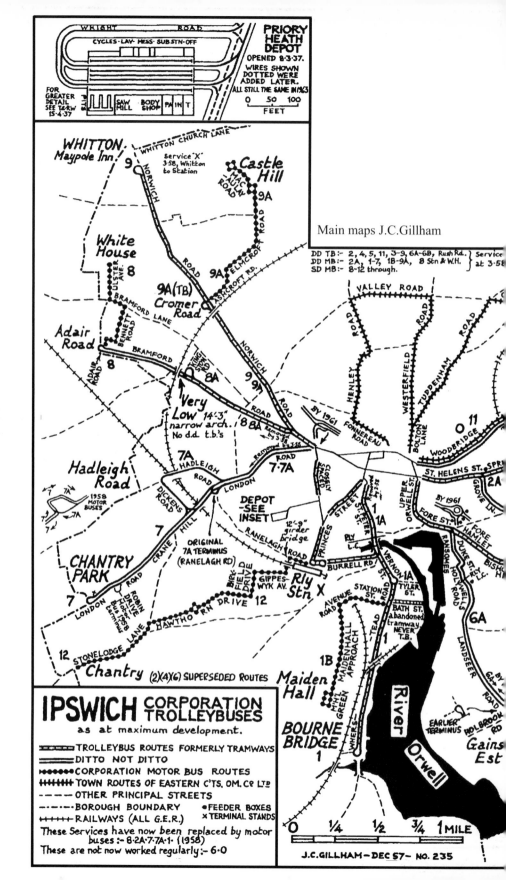

PRIORY HEATH DEPOT

WRIGHT ROAD
CYCLES·LAV·MESS·SUB·STN·OFF
SAW MILL · BODY SHOP · PAINT

FOR GREATER DETAIL SEE T&RW 15·4·37

OPENED 8·3·37.
WIRES SHOWN DOTTED WERE ADDED LATER.
ALL STILL THE SAME IN 1963.

0   50   100
FEET

WHITTON. Maypole Inn   9
WHITTON CHURCH LANE
Service 'X' 3·58, Whitton to Station

Castle Hill   9A

MAC AULAY ROAD
ELMCROFT ROAD

Main maps J.C.Gillham

DD TB:- 2, 4, 5, 11, 3-9, 6A-6B, Rush Rd. } Service
DD MB:- 2A, 1-7, 1B-9A, 8 Stn & W.H.   } at 3·58
SD MB:- 8-12 through.

White House   8
ULSTER AVE.

NORWICH ROAD

9A ELMCROFT
SASCROFT RD.

9A(TB) Cromer Road

VALLEY ROAD

Adair Road   8
BRAMFORD LANE
BENNETT ROAD

BRAMFORD

ADAIR ROAD

HENLEY ROAD
WESTERFIELD ROAD
TUDDENHAM ROAD
BOLTON LANE

WOODBRIDGE   O 11

8A   9 9A

NORWICH ROAD

BY 1961
FONNEREAU ROAD

Very Low 14'3" narrow arch.. No d.d. t.b.'s
8 8A
8 8A Removed by 3·58

ST. HELENS ST. SPRI

2A

7A HADLEIGH ROAD
Removed by 3·58
ROAD 7·7A

Hadleigh Road
1958 MOTOR BUSES   7A   7A   7A

CLOSELY SPACED
BY 1961
FORE ST.
FORE HAMLET

PRINCES STREET
STREET ST.

1 1A

UPPER ORWELL ST.

GROVE LN

DICKENS ROAD

CRANE HILL

ROAD   LONDON

DEPOT -SEE INSET

12'9" girder bridge

RANELAGH ROAD

RLY L.C.

VERNON 1A
1A

DUKE ST.
RANSOMES
HOLYWELL'S ROAD
BISHO

7
CHANTRY PARK

ORIGINAL 7A TERMINUS (RANELAGH RD)

BIRK FIELD DRIVE
GIPPES WYK AV.

BURRELL RD.

Rly Stn X

STATION ST.

1A TYLER ST.

6A
LANDSEER

7
LONDON ROAD

ROBIN DRIVE 1958 bus terminus

HAWTHORN DRIVE   12

STONELODGE LANE

12   Chantry (2X4X6) SUPERSEDED ROUTES

AVENUE ROAD

STEAD ROAD

BATH ST. abandoned tramway NEVER T.B.

MILL GREEN
MAIDENHALL APPROACH

1B
Maiden Hall

1

EARLIER TERMINUS

HOLBROOK RD.
BY 6A

Gains Est.

River Orwell

IPSWICH CORPORATION TROLLEYBUSES
as at maximum development.

═══ TROLLEYBUS ROUTES FORMERLY TRAMWAYS
════ DITTO NOT DITTO
•••• CORPORATION MOTOR BUS ROUTES
++++ TOWN ROUTES OF EASTERN C'TS. OM. Cᵒ LTD
- - - OTHER PRINCIPAL STREETS
-·-·- BOROUGH BOUNDARY   • FEEDER BOXES
++++ RAILWAYS (ALL G.E.R.)   × TERMINAL STANDS

These Services have now been replaced by motor buses :- 8·2A·7·7A·1· (1958)
These are not now worked regularly :- 6·0

BOURNE BRIDGE   1
WHERS

0   ¼   ½   ¾   1 MILE

J.C.GILLHAM - DEC 57 - NO. 235

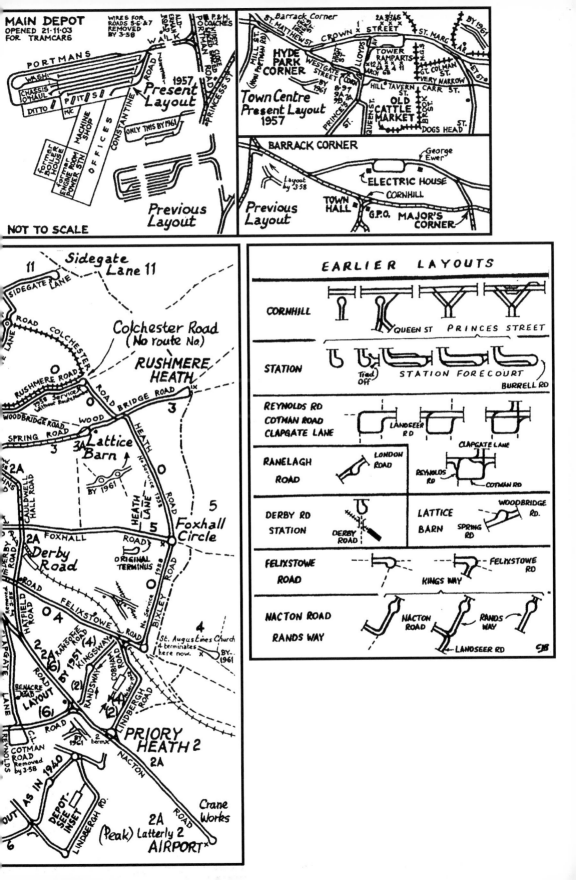

GEOGRAPHICAL SETTING

From the earliest days Ipswich has always been linked to the River Orwell with its access to the East Coast, North Sea and the near continent. In Saxon times a settlement was established in the area where the River Orwell was fordable.

Ipswich developed as a trading port but stagnated in the eighteenth century. All this changed in the nineteenth century when the river channel was dredged and realigned and the docks developed thus changing this provincial market town, with its decaying port, into an industrial town with busy shipping activity.

The industrial development tended to be in the dock/river area and included manufacturing companies of worldwide fame including Ransomes Sims & Jefferies plus Ransomes & Rapier. Other substantial industries included agricultural fertilisers, milling and malting.

The advent of the railway from London to Colchester in 1846, plus the lines to Bury St Edmunds and Norwich in 1846 and 1849, greatly improved transport facilities in the area although the original and current railway station are some way from the town centre.

This rapid development lead to substantial increases in population as people from the country areas moved to the town in search of employment. Thus, by the late nineteenth century, the need for some form of public transport was becoming apparent if the town was to continue to develop.

The terrain around Ipswich is by no means flat and the steepest gradients for trolleybuses were Bishops Hill, Grove Lane and the Woodbridge, Spring and St Johns Roads.

HISTORICAL BACKGROUND

The first privately owned horse drawn tramway in Ipswich was opened on 13th October 1880 from Cornhill to the Railway Station with a further route opened along Norwich Road from Princes Street via Portman Road, Mill Street and Barrack Corner to Brooks Hall Road in March 1881. During this year the tramway company was incorporated by Act of Parliament and in August 1882 the connection was made between Barrack Corner and Cornhill. In the summer of 1883 the section from Majors Corner to Derby Road station was opened and in June 1884 the gap in the system between Cornhill and Majors Corner was opened for service thus completing the extent of the horse tramways in the town. In 1898 the horse tramway saw competition from the red horse buses of the "Ipswich Omnibus Service" who opened up routes to various parts of the town.

Having obtained powers to establish an electricity undertaking in 1897, the 1900 Ipswich Corporation Tramway Act authorised the running of electric trams and the horse tramway company was acquired by compulsory purchase for £17,552 with the municipality taking over operations on 1st November 1901. A committee was appointed to co-ordinate the introduction of both the electric light supply to the town and the construction of the electric tramway; a 7-acre (2.8 hectare) field in Constantine Road was the site

chosen for the erection of the power station, tram depot/workshops and refuse destruction plant.

Horse trams ceased on 6th June 1903 to allow track to be laid to a 3'6" gauge (1067mm) and an initial order for 26 trams was placed with Brush of Loughborough. The first public service opened on 23rd November 1903 from Whitton to Bourne Bridge with a branch along Bath Street to cater for the Great Eastern Railway river steamers. Various routes were converted and new ones opened which lead to the demise of the competing horse buses by the end of 1903. The last route to be opened was along Felixstowe Road in May 1904 by which time an additional 10 cars had been delivered.

Like the majority of tramway systems the 1914-18 war took its toll with lack of materials for track and vehicle maintenance that was compounded by many of the male employees being required for war service. After the war the track was in a particularly poor state and although some was replaced the management began to consider "trackless trams", i.e. trolleybuses.

A pilot project was introduced with 3 single deck vehicles hired from Railless Limited of Rochester and used from Cornhill to Ipswich Station. The service opened on 2nd September 1923 and was such a success that tram track along the majority of Princes Street was lifted and the road resurfaced in the spring of 1924. A further single deck vehicle was purchased from Ransomes Sims & Jefferies (RSJ) in 1924.

In 1925 the Corporation obtained an Act of Parliament that allowed them to replace the trams with trolleybuses. Despite some opposition from those who preferred the use of motorbuses the attraction of using municipally generated power from what was in effect the same operating department influenced the positive outcome of a local referendum on the subject. The Wherstead Road (Bourne Bridge) via Stoke Bridge route was converted on 17th July 1925 to allow trials with a number of demonstration vehicles following which orders were placed for 30 single deck vehicles split equally between RSJ and Garretts of Leiston and these were delivered during the Spring/Summer of 1926.

The next route to be converted was Felixstowe Road that opened on 27th May 1926 and extended beyond the Royal Oak tram terminus to Kings Way. The next month the Spring Road to Lattice Barn and St Johns Road/Cauldwell Hall Road to Derby Road Station was opened on 9th June. The 27th July saw the opening of the Whitton and Bramford Road routes with the latter being extended under the low railway bridge to Adair Road. The last trams had run on the preceding day. There had been many months of intense activity by the overhead erection teams to enable these routes to be converted in a three month period.

The Foxhall Road route was introduced temporarily to Derby Road Station on 22nd December 1926 and to the original terminus just beyond the hospital on 29th March 1927. On the latter date the route from Barrack Corner along London Road to the junction with Ranelagh Road commenced. There was then a twelve month gap before the next extension, which was from Derby Road station across Felixstowe Road at the Royal Oak, along Hatfield and Nacton Roads to Rands Way and along Kings Way to join up with the terminus of the Felixstowe Road route. This was opened on 18th March 1928.

A route into the developing Gainsborough Estate was opened on 28th July 1931 by wiring the rest of Nacton Road from Bishops Hill to Hatfield Road and from the junction with Rands Way along Landseer Road to terminate with a "round the houses" movement at Reynolds Road. To meet increasing traffic the first double deck trolleybuses were introduced in 1933.

It was nearly three years before the next extension that was from Lattice Barn to Rushmere

Heath opening on 25th April 1934. One month later the London Road route was extended to serve the Royal Agricultural Show that opened on 16th May 1934 with the trolleybus fleet providing trojan service in moving the majority of the visitors to and from the showground. To facilitate this a new town centre terminus was opened at Electric House with wiring to Hyde Park Corner.

On 6th December 1936 a major extension was opened from Electric House along Woodbridge, Rushmere, Colchester, Heath, Bixley and Felixstowe Roads to join with the existing system at Kings Way. On the same date connection was made from Electric House to Majors Corner and seven days later the Foxhall Road route was extended the short distance to the junction with Bixley Road hence joining up with the extension indicated above.

In 1937 a new depot and workshop facility was opened at Priory Heath off Cobham Road. There was no further expansion until thirteen months later when on 30th January 1938 wiring was opened along Landseer Road from Reynolds Road to the junction with Holbrook Road. Later in the year on 31st October a single loop off London Road was opened via Dickens and Hadleigh Roads.

On 23rd April 1939 the Nacton Road route was extended as far as Lindbergh Road and along same to Cobham Road thereby joining existing wiring servicing the Priory Heath depot. Rands Way and Kings Way journeys ceased although unconnected wiring was left in place for supply purposes and the Kings Way destination used later for Priory Heath depot workings.

There was one extension during the 1939-1945 war which left Fore Street to travel along Duke Street and Holywells/Landseer Roads to join up with the existing wiring at Holbrook Road; this was opened on 26th February 1940. In 1942 the majority of the aging overhead wiring and fittings were replaced with profiled wire and 24" (610mm) spaced components supplied by British Insulated Cables the forerunner of British Insulated Calendars Cables (BICC). This allowed the use of carbon insert skates instead of trolley wheels for electric current collection.

Immediately after the war route extensions were planned and implemented. On 17th December 1945 Clapgate Lane from Nacton Road to Landseer Road was opened and on 10th April 1947 the Sidegate Lane route was introduced. Later that year on 17th August the

Nacton Road wiring was extended to the Airport; this was the last extension apart from changes enforced by town centre traffic management schemes and construction of the short working turning circle on Bramford Road at the junction with Kingston Road (1950).

In 1949 a westbound one-way system was introduced along Carr, Tavern and Westgate Streets and thus Lloyds Avenue was wired from Electric House to Cornhill (10th July 1949) to allow vehicles to reach the southern routes along Princes and Queen Streets. Vehicles travelling westward along Westgate Street could either continue into St Matthews Street to Barrack Corner or turn into Crown Street at Hyde Park Corner to reach the Electric House stands. These arrangements bought the system to its maximum of 25.5 route miles (41km).

Although the immediate post-war expansion seemed to bode well for this all trolleybus system there were factors that were beginning to move against this type of vehicle. The transport and electricity functions had always been operated as a single integrated department but in 1948 the electricity industry was nationalised by the newly elected Labour government and thus passed out of Ipswich's ownership. The new Cliff Quay Generating Station was started by Ipswich Corporation but was under the new ownership when opened in 1949 thus eventually replacing the original power station at Constantine Road. Ipswich therefore no longer had control over the cost of electricity supplied to the trolleybus system.

New post-war housing estates were being built and the council decided to use motorbuses for the first time to service these new residential areas with the initial route opening on 4th May 1950 to the Whitehouse Estate. This was the beginning of the end for the trolleybuses since in the post-war period there was only a limited number of vehicle manufacturers and the closure, or the proposed closure of other systems (particularly London Transport), lead to overhead equipment suppliers and chassis manufacturers gradually withdrawing from the market.

In 1951 some trolleybus services were withdrawn including the eastern circular routes plus regular services using Portman Road and in 1953 new single decker motorbuses replaced the ubiquitous single deck trolleybuses along Bramford Road. Motorbuses gradually replaced trolleybuses on all routes until the final journey on 23rd August 1963. So ended 60 years of electric traction on the streets of Ipswich of which the trolleybus had contributed 40 years of service.

Although the system had finished the vehicles had not with eight from the last delivery being sold for further service to Walsall Corporation in 1962. Seven were later absorbed into the West Midlands Passenger Transport Executive in 1969 and withdrawn in 1970.

TRAMS TO TROLLEYBUSES

1.   One of the three original Railless trolleybuses is about to negotiate the Cornhill turning circle before returning along Princes Street on the right and onwards to the Station on the opening experimental route. Tram 1 awaits departure to Lattice Barn with the motorman perhaps wondering if the "trackless" will be a success and whether he will be able to adapt to the driving techniques required on this new type of vehicle.
(Commercial Postcard/Ipswich Transport Museum)

2.   The old and the new.   Ransomes trolleybus 12 picks up passengers at the Royal Oak on Felixstowe Road whilst three trams, headed by 27, are parked awaiting disposal with some earlier withdrawals already having been sold to the Scarborough Tramways Company. Although the front entrance of 12 is open passengers also appear to be boarding via the rear exit. Also note the electrical feeder box in the foreground. (R Markham collection)

ELECTRIC HOUSE

3. The Electric House town centre terminus was around the perimeter of a car park flanked by the Tower Ramparts School to the south and the office block that comprised Electric House to the west. The car park is now the Tower Ramparts Bus Station. In this view Ransomes 86 is seen using the south side overhead passing loop in May 1958 whilst on the Felixstowe Road circular Route 0. The building to the rear currently houses Yates's pub and restaurant. (R Marshall)

Timetable December 1939. Note the early time of the last wartime departures.

From ELECTRIC HOUSE

TO Colchester Road	Woodbridge Road Circular to Foxhall Road		Felixstowe Road Circular to Foxhall Rd. Circus		4 To Kingsway		6 To Gainsboro' Estate		7a To Hadleigh Road	
Weekdays	Week days	Suns	Week days	Suns	Week days	Suns	Week days	Sats	Week days	Suns
a.m.	a.m.	a.m.	a.m.	a.m.	a.m.	a.m.	a.m.	a.m.	a.m.	a.m.
6 56	6 56	9 51	6 27	9 45	6 27	9 45	6 35	6 35	6 40	9 31
7 4	7 12	1011	6 43	10 5	6 43	10 5	6 51	6 40	6 45	9 41
Then	7 28	1031	6 59	1025	6 51	1015	7 3	6 45	6 55	9 51
every	7 44	1051	7 15	1045	6 59	1025	7 19	6 50	7 3	Then
8	8 0	1111	7 31	11 5	7 7	1035 ⌉	7 28	6 55	7 11	every
mins.	8 16	1131	7 47	1125	7 15	1045	7 35	7 0	7 19	10
until	8 32	1151	Then	1145	7 23	1055 ⌋	7 43	7 5	7 27	mins.
p.m.	8 48	Then	every	Then	7 31	Then	7 51	7 10	7 35	until
6 8	Then	every	16	every	7 39	every	7 59	7 20	Then	p.m.
6 15	every	20	mins.	20	7 47	10	Then	Then	every	7 7
6 24	16	mins.	until	mins.	7 55	mins.	every	every	8	......
6 32	mins.	until	p.m.	until	Then	until	8	5	mins.	......
6 39	until	p.m.	6 11	p.m.	every	p.m.	mins.	mins.	until	......
6 48	p.m.	6 51	6 27	6 45	8	7 5	until	until	p.m.	......
6 56	6 8	7 1	6‡43	7 5	mins.	7 15	7 3	1115	6 7	......
7 4	6 24	7 11	6 55	7‡17	until	7 17	7 11	1120	6 15	......
7 16	6 39	7 21	7‡10	......	p.m.	......	7 22	1124	6 23	......
7 24	6 56	7 25	7‡26	......	6 11	......	Then	1128	6 31	......
7 36	7 16	......	......	......	6 19	......	4	Then	6 47	......
	7 24				6 27		mins.	4	6 56	
Sundays	7 36				6 33		Fris	mins.	7 3	
a.m.					6 43		same	until	7 16	
9 51					6 49		as	p.m.		
Then					6 55		Wdys	7 20		
every					7 0		until	7 22		
10					7 10		a.m.	7 26		
mins.					7 26		1127			
until							1135	Suns.		
p.m.							1142	a.m.		
6 51							1149	9 50		
7 1							1154	Then		
7 11							12 0	every		
7 21							p.m.	10		
7 25							12 6	mins.		
							1212	until		
							1218	p.m.		
							1224	1 40		
							1230	1 48		
							Then	1 56		
							every	Then		
							6	every		
							mins.	6		
							until	mins.		
							7 12	until		
							7 20	7 16		
							7 22			

‡–Kingsway only.

4.   The Tower Ramparts School building on the right forms the background to this June 1951 view with three trolleybuses awaiting departure from the south side. In the foreground is Ransomes 57 on Route 4 to Kings Way. Note the nearside cab door and the cables on the centre front roof feeding power from the overhead down into the cab area. To the rear are two post war Sunbeams with the front vehicle and 57 on the nearside wiring. A Ford Prefect car bonnet can be seen in the immediate foreground. (R Marshall)

5.   Ransomes 46 turns into the west side of the terminus and will complete a further right turn to travel along the north side as it leaves for Priory Heath. The exit from the passing loop in front of the school can be seen on the right and the overhead wiring leaving the top of the picture leads into Lloyds Avenue. Egertons garage, which was demolished to make way for the Crown Swimming Pools, is to the immediate left. (C Carter)

6.   An immediate post war view of Ransomes single decker 18, new in 1926, entering the north side of the terminus from Crown Street with Egertons garage as the backdrop. It is destined for the short working Route 3A to Lattice Barn and has lining out, ITC logo, bulb horn and is devoid of roof mounted advertising boards which were added to similar vehicles. Note the tops of the booms are angled to allow for the use of the carbon insert collectors used on double deck vehicles. (W J Haynes)

7.   This view looks west along the north side in October 1961 with the Tower Ramparts School buildings on the left, Electric House in the centre and The Cricketers public house on the right. Karrier 110 stands under the nearside set of parallel wiring leading from Crown Street in the background; the offside wiring completed the turning manoeuvre around the car park. The overhead junction in the foreground allowed vehicles using either set of wiring to move to the south side of the terminus. (J C Gillham)

8.   Over 14 years separate these two vehicles photographed in 1951 adjacent to the Foxhall Road stand with the school buildings in the background. Ransomes 62, delivered in 1936, awaits departure on Route 5 to Foxhall Road with Sunbeam 124 dating from 1950 immediately behind and destined for Rushmere Heath. The change in design over the years has deleted the piano front, nearside cab door and mid position side destination indicator. 124 was sold to Walsall Corporation in 1962 and became their 345. (J C Gillham)

9. Karrier W 96 turns out of Crown Street into Tower Street, which formed the eastern side of the Electric House terminus, in March 1958. In the background is the Bethesda Baptist Church whilst the naval ratings stand under a sign that is a testimony to the then British car industry. (J C Gillham)

10. Ransomes 61 is seen in Tower Street in July 1952 immediately before turning right towards the Tower Ramparts School buildings. A Leyland PS coach moves westerly along Crown Street whilst the Carnaby Street influence on female dress style is still some way off! (J H Meredith)

LLOYDS AVENUE

11.   The short length of Lloyds Avenue connected Electric House to the Cornhill and was wired in this direction on the introduction of the westerly one way system along Carr, Tavern and Westgate Streets in 1949. This connection allowed vehicles from Crown Street/Electric House access to Princes and Queen Streets. Rebuilt single decker 37 waits at the top of Lloyds Avenue before departing on Route 1A to Tyler Street which was a short working of the Bourne Bridge service. Note the crews are in their summer uniforms and also the solid runners between the twin line hangers and the junction in the overhead wiring. (C Carter)

12. A little further down Lloyds Avenue Ransomes 75 waits prior to departure on Route 1 to Bourne Bridge in June 1951. In the background is the overhead wiring from the Electric House terminus with Egertons garage beyond. (R Marshall)

→ 13. Ransomes 65 emerges from under the archway at the bottom of Lloyds Avenue and prepares to cross Cornhill to enter Princes Street on its way to the Station. This vehicle is one of the early Ransomes double deckers that had the front end modified by the Corporation which provided for a deeper windscreen. (D A Jones/London Trolleybus Preservation Society)

CORNHILL

14.   The stands on the western side of Cornhill serviced the routes exiting from the town via Westgate Street and here a Park Royal bodied utility Karrier W 97 waits for passengers before leaving on Route 9A to Norwich Road Bridge, a short working of the Whitton service. The black and white kerb markings are a leftover of the wartime blackout restrictions and Brett's Furniture Store continues to trade. This view was taken during 1950 after the introduction of the one way system in Carr, Tavern and Westgate Streets. (C Carter)

⟶ 15.This pre-war view of Ransomes 38 clearly shows the verandah type platform and half cab construction to allow for one man pay as you enter operation. The Corporation later rebuilt this batch of vehicles with full fronts and the entrance covered; see Picture 49 for a comparison. 38 is on a short working of the London Road service to Hadleigh Road designated Route 7A. Given that the Transport and Electricity Departments were effectively one unit the advertisement extolling the virtues of gas seems inappropriate. Does anyone in the Ipswich area recognise the couple on the right? (J Fielder/R Marshall)

⟶ 16.This Karrier W delivered in 1948 has a stylish Park Royal body when compared with the earlier utility designs from the same body builder. Passengers wait to board 108 destined for Whitton as it stands under the nearside set of parallel wiring, with the offside overhead providing a passing loop. Note the sign hanging from the standard in front of the office block that gives directions to the Natural History Museum and Public Baths in this 1950 view. The sign is now on display at the Ipswich Transport Museum. (C Carter)

17.   This view dates from the mid 1930s with Burton's store under construction and Ransomes double decker 55 awaiting departure to the Gainsborough Estate; the wiring in the foreground leads into Princes Street. Note the advertisement for Imperial Typewriters.
(Ipswich Transport Museum)

18. A pre-war view on the eastern side of Cornhill as Ransomes 16, dating from 1926, picks up passengers for Route 1 to Bourne Bridge under wiring that leads from Tavern Street into Princes Street. Note the fare stage/bus stop on the right and the exterior mounted lighting for the destination indicator. The building on the left with a tower like structure was the Picture House cinema. (Omnibus Society)

Timetable December 1939. Note the early times of the last wartime departures.

From CORNHILL

3a — To Lattice Barn, Week days a.m.	Suns a.m.	5 — To Foxhall Road, Week days a.m.	Suns a.m.	8 — To Bramford Road, Week days a.m.	Suns a.m.	9 — To Whitton, Week days a.m.	Suns a.m.	9a — To Norwich Rd. Bridge, Week days a.m.	Suns a.m.	X — To Ipswich Station, Week days a.m.	Suns a.m.
6 42	9 51	6 47	9 52	6 51	9 44	6 27	9 44	6 27	9 44	7 22	9 20
6 58	9 58	6 52	Then	6 56	9 51	6 39	9 51	6 39	9 51	7 27	9 35
7 8	10 5	6 57	at	7 1	9 58	6 55	9 58	6 55	9 58	7 32	9 45
7 18	1019	7 2	2 32	7 6	10 5	7 5	10 5	7 5	10 5	7 37	9 49
7 23	1026	7 12	12 42	7 11	1012	7 12	1019	7 12	1012	7 42	9 54
7 28	1033	7 22	22 52	7 16	1019	7 15	1033	7 15	1019	7 47	10 5
7 33	1040	7 32	mins.	7 21	1026	7 30	1047	7 30	1026	7 57	1012
7 38	1047	7 37	each	7 26	1033	7 44	11 1	7 37	1033	Then	1019
7 43	1054	7 42	hour	7 31	1040	7 52	Then	7 44	1040	every	1026
7 48	11 1	7 47	until	7 36	1047	Then	every	7 47	1047	5	1033
7 53	Then	7 52	6 12	7 41	1054	at	14	7 52	1054	mins.	1040
7 58	every	7 57	6 22	7 46	Then	mins.	mins.	7 57	Then	until	1047
Then	7	Then	6 32	7 51	every	past	until	Then	every	p.m.	1054
every	mins.	every	6 42	7 56	7	each	1 35	every	mins.	7 7	Then
5	until	5	6 52	Then	mins.	hour	1 49	5	until	7 11	7
mins.	p.m.	mins.	7 2	every	until	until	2 0	mins.	p.m.	7 16	mins.
until	5 19	until	7 12	5	p.m.	p.m.	2 3	until	1 49	7 28	until
p.m.	5 26	p.m.	7 22	mins.	6 1	7 2	2 10	p.m.	1 56		p.m.
6 33	5 33	7 2		until	6 8	7 14	2 17	7 2	2 0		6 43
6 40	5 40	7 7		p.m.	6 15	7 20	2 24	7 7	2 3		6 50
6 45	5 47	7 11		6 56	6 22	Sats a.m.	2 31	7 14	2 10		6 57
6 52	5 54	7 17		7 1	6 29	6 27	2 38	7 20	2 24		7 4
6 58	6 1	7 20		7 7	6 36	6 39	2 45		2 31		7 11
7 1	6 8	7 26		7 13	6 43	6 55	Then		2 38		7 18
7 5	6 15			7 22	6 50	7 5	every		Then		7 25
7 11	6 22			7 25	6 57	7 12	7		every		
7 17	6 29				7 4	7 15	mins.		7		
7 23	6 36				7 11	7 27	until		mins.		
	6 43					7 30	p.m.		until		
	6 50					7 37	6 50		p.m.		
	6 57					7 44	6 57		7 4		
	7 4					7 47	7 11		7 11		
	7 11					7 52	7 18		7 18		
	7 18					Then					
						every					
						5 mins					
						until					
						p.m.					
						7 7					
						7 14					
						7 20					

19.   The conductor chats to his driver through the nearside door of Ransomes 84 at the same location in the mid 1940s prior to departing for Bourne Bridge. The painting of the passenger queue corridor and destination on the pavement, a common practice in Ipswich, was unusual elsewhere. The Picture House cinema can again be seen in the background. (W J Haynes)

PRINCES STREET

20.   Having turned round in the Cornhill Railless 3 from the original batch of trolleybuses awaits departure to the Station from the stand at the head of Princes Street. The view dates from 1923-25 with tram tracks still in place and the stop/stage sign mounted on the standard to the rear. Also note the clerestory roof reminiscent of early railway carriage design. (Omnibus Society)

21.   Ransomes 18 passes the Princes Street/Queen Street junction on its way to the Station. This view was probably taken not long after the vehicle's introduction in May 1926 as it passes over redundant tram track and with the route number box without a blind that was fitted later. Also note the slip board beneath the nearside windscreen displaying "Ipswich Station". The solid tyres were subsequently changed to pneumatic as depicted in Picture 6. (Author's collection. Commercial Postcard)

22.   Railless 2 passes the end of Portman Road as it makes its way along Princes Street to the town centre. The trial with trolleybuses was a success and the Corporation wasted no time in removing tram track along most of Princes Street as indicated by the workmen's activities. The houses on the right are no more and form the site of Staples Stationery store. (Ipswich Transport Museum)

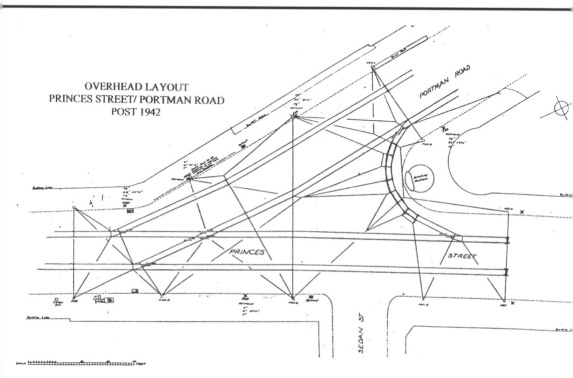

OVERHEAD LAYOUT
PRINCES STREET/ PORTMAN ROAD
POST 1942

23.   Seen on a private hire duty for an enthusiasts' tour Sunbeam 126 reaches the end of Princes Street and the bridge over the River Orwell with the left hand semaphore indicator in position ready for the turn into Burrell Road. An inspector waits to board to check all is well when the tour starts from the Station in January 1961. (D Mackley)

BURRELL ROAD/STATION/ STOKE STREET

24.   Sunbeam 117 leaves the parallel wiring in front of the station forecourt as it turns into Princes Street on its way to Foxhall Road. Note the second set of parallel wiring on the left in front of the Station Hotel that was removed well before the closure of the system and the Eastern Counties Bristol single decker in the background. (W J Haynes)

→ 25. At the same location in July 1952 Ransomes 52 turns into Princes Street with destination blinds still showing Station X (i.e. 10); as there are no passengers perhaps 52 is returning to Constantine Road depot via Portman Road. The overhead junction for the unused wiring along the rest of Burrell Road can be seen in the background and there is now only a single set of wiring in front of the Station Hotel. (J H Meredith)

→ 26. This scene at the stand in front of the station forecourt depicts Ransomes single decker 38 in front of a wartime Karrier W with utility body. 38 was originally delivered with verandah front entrance and half cab but was subsequently rebuilt with full front by the Corporation as shown. Both vehicles are on the nearside wiring and advertising boards have not been fitted to the single decker. The waste land to the left is now the station multi-storey car park. (R Marshall)

Timetable December 1939. Note the early times of last wartime departures.

9 & 9a Ipswich Stn. to Norwich Rd. Bridge		X Norwich Rd. Bge. to Ipswich Station		X Foxhall Road to Ipswich Station	X Rushmere Heath to Ipswich Station	X Whitton to Ipswich Station	
Week days	Suns	Week days	Suns	Weekdays	Sundays only	Sats	Suns
a.m.	a.m.	a.m.	a.m.	a.m.	a.m.	a.m.	p.m.
7 34	1014	7 28	10 9	6†36	1012	7 25	2 16
7 44	1020	Then	1023	7 6	1026	7 34	2 30
7 54	1027	every	1037	7 16	1040	7 44	2 44
Then	1034	10	1051	Then	1054	7 54	2 58
every	1041	mins.	11 5	every	11 8	8 4	3 12
10	1048	until	1119	10	1122	Then	3 26
mins.	1052	p.m.	1133	mins.	1136	every	3 40
until	11 2	1258	1147	until	1150	10	3 54
p.m.	11 9	1 18	12 1	p.m.	p.m.	mins.	4 8
1 14	1116	1 28	1215	6 56	12 4	until	4 22
1 34	1123	Then	1229	7†15	1218	p.m.	4 36
Then	1130	every	1243	......	1232	6 34	4 50
every	1137	10	1257	......	1246	6 41	5 4
10	1144	mins.	1 11	......	1 0	6 54	5 18
mins.	1151	until	1 25	......	1 14	7 3	5 32
until	1158	6 28	1 39	......	1 28	7 15	5 46
7 14	Then	6 38	1 53	......	1 42	7†25	6 0
7†22	7	6 45	2 7	......	1 56	7†32	6 14
7†34	until	6 58	2 21	......	2 10	......	6 28
......	mins.	7 7	2 35	......	2 24	......	6 42
......	p.m.	7 19	2 49	......	2 38	......	6 56
......	6 58	7†36	3 3	......	2 52	......	7 10
......	7 5	......	3 17	......	3 6	......	7†24
......	7 12	......	3 31	......	3 20	......	7†34
......	7†21	......	3 45	......	3 34	......	......
......	7†33	......	3 59	......	3 48	......	......
......	......	......	4 13	......	Then		
......	......	......	4 27	......	every		
......	......	......	4 41	......	14		
......	......	......	4 55	......	mins.		
......	......	......	5 9	......	until		
......	......	......	5 23	......	7 4		
......	......	......	5 37	......	7†18		
......	......	......	5 51				
......	......	......	6 5				
......	......	......	6 19				
......	......	......	6 33				
......	......	......	6 47				
......	......	......	7 1				
......	......	......	7 15				
......	......	......	7†29				
......	......	......	7†39				

†—To Cornhill only.

27.   At the same location Ransomes 61 awaits departure to Whitton with a single decker for Adair Road in the foreground and a further vehicle parked under the overhead junction for the passing loop. The wiring for the turning circle can be seen on the left; also note the use of the nearside cab door on 61. (A D Packer)

28. Ransomes 86 is seen in Stoke Street outside Stoke Hall on an enthusiasts' tour in July 1949. This part of Stoke Street formed a short extension of Burrell Road leading down to Stoke Bridge. The overhead wiring from the station along Burrell Road to Stoke Bridge was never used other than for special workings and system tours with the wiring to the rear of 86 "tied off" and not physically connected to the overhead of the Bourne Bridge route; it did however provide an electrical supply between the two locations. The original reason for wiring this stretch was to provide a link from the station to Wherstead Road and thence to Bourne Bridge whilst Stoke Bridge was being rebuilt in 1924/25. Although wiring was installed it was not used and two trams were used to provide a shuttle service until the Bourne Bridge route was converted to trolleybuses. (J H Meredith)

STOKE BRIDGE/WHERSTEAD ROAD/ BOURNE BRIDGE

29.   Park Royal bodied Sunbeam 120 is seen in Bridge Street passing over the railway track that leads to the dockside in front of Cranfield's buildings on the right. The crossing was used by a steam tram engine to move wagons from the dock area to marshalling sidings. A single track is still in place with appropriate warning signs but the left side opposite the docks was overgrown with shrubs until recently. The tower of St Peters Church can be seen in the background. (J H Meredith)

⟶ 30.Ransomes 13, which appears to be on test, crosses the newly built Stoke Bridge over the River Orwell and enters Vernon Street on its way to Wherstead Road and the Bourne Bridge terminus. In the background the British Fermentation Products factory site is now covered by the roadway of the later second bridge and a skateboard park. Although the registration number appears to be 5814 it is in fact 5614. (S Lockwood collection)

⟶ 31.Having travelled along Wherstead Road we are now at the terminus just short of Bourne Bridge with Ransomes single decker 20 (complete with burnished aluminium panels after rebuilding) having used the tight turning circle ready for the return to town and thence onward to Adair Road. This view clearly shows the three step entrance and good use of revenue generating advertising boards. Waiting to turn is Ransomes 86 on an enthusiasts' special.
(A D Packer)

WESTGATE STREET/HYDE PARK CORNER

32.   In this view Sunbeam 126 has just crossed the Museum/High Street junction as it makes its way along Westgate Street towards Hyde Park Corner and thence onwards to Norwich Road and Whitton in October 1961. The junction of the parallel overhead wiring on the one way system from Cornhill can be clearly seen together with The Barley Mow public house that is now the site of an Ann Summers shop. (J C Gillham)

33.   This view looks at Hyde Park Corner from St Matthews Street. The trolleybus on the right is about to leave Westgate Street on its way to Whitton whilst the vehicle on the left rounds the bend into Crown Street and onwards to Rushmere Heath although the rear destination blind has not been changed. A British Road Services delivery van, a Ford Anglia and a Morris Minor convertible complete this October 1961 scene. (J C Gillham)

ST MATTHEWS STREET/
BARRACK CORNER

34.   Looking along St Matthews Street from Hyde Park Corner in October 1961 Karrier 110 waits at the traffic lights before bearing left into Crown Street on route to Rushmere Heath. Amongst the properties on view note The Rainbow pub on the right and Smith's Albion House store on the corner of Lady Lane on the left. All is now demolished apart from two buildings beyond Albion House. In the top right of the picture the splicing ears in the overhead can be seen where the crossover has been removed which took wiring from Westgate Street into Crown Street. (J C Gillham)

35.　　A snowy scene in St Matthews Street taken in the late 1920s with Garrett 21 overtaking a car of the period as it makes its way towards Hyde Park Corner. The route number box has no blind and the slip board under the nearside windscreen indicates the destination. The scene is unrecognisable today; the traffic island at the top of Civic Drive is roughly where the building with the Pooles advertisement stands. (Ipswich Transport Museum)

36.　　Wartime utility Karrier W 90 leaves St Matthews Street to enter Norwich Road at Barrack Corner with the Half Moon and Star public house on the left; this is now a private residence. The wiring in the top right hand corner is from London Road. Also note the pre-war tradition of a centrally positioned side destination blind; the author is not sure whether this was fitted from new or added at a later date but the latter is the more likely. (W J Haynes)

37.   Barrack Corner with inward bound Karrier W 103 leaving Norwich Road and entering St Matthews Street. The overhead wiring branching to the left leads into London Road and that leaving the extreme left gave access to Portman Road. The overhead connection between Portman Road to the outward bound Norwich Road wiring has been removed in this April 1953 view. The road in the centre is Clarkson Street and the Half Moon and Star pub is on the extreme right. (A D Packer)

38.   Karrier 109 enters Barrack Corner from Portman Road (this section was originally Mill Street) and will complete a sharp right hand turn into St Matthews Street and thence to the Crown Street/Electric House stand for Foxhall Road. (W J Haynes)

LONDON ROAD/HADLEIGH ROAD

39.   Jack's transport drivers' accommodation was ideally situated next to the British Road Services depot in Hadleigh Road. Ransomes 62 is just about to complete the single line loop from London Road via Dickens Road on its return to town. The area to the rear is now occupied by the Sainsbury's store.
(H Luff/Online Transport Archive/Photobus)

———➤ 40.After a dewirement, or taking the wrong overhead line, the conductor of Ransomes 80 places the boom on the correct wiring leading from London Road into Dickens Road. 80 can now complete the circuit round the single loop into Hadleigh Road and back to London Road for the return trip to town.
(G Austin/Ipswich Transport Museum)

———➤ 41.Ransomes 86 is seen again, this time at the London Road terminus, whilst on an enthusiasts' tour of the system; the shadow of the turning circle wiring can be seen on the roadway. The route was extended from Ranelagh Road to this point in 1934 to provide public transport to the Royal Show that was held on adjacent land. The lack of traffic on the single carriageway next to Chantry Park on the left is difficult to believe by today's standards.
(D A Jones/London Trolleybus Preservation Society)

NORWICH ROAD/ WHITTON

42. Ransomes 81 is about to leave Norwich Road and turn Barrack Corner into St Matthews Street on Route 3 to Rushmere Heath. The shop on the right still deals in ladies' fashions but is now under new ownership. (W J Haynes)

43.   Ipswich Corporation allowed Ransomes to test vehicles they had produced for other operators on the local system. St Helens Corporation 111 is seen here under the Norwich Road railway bridge that carries track to Felixstowe and the East Suffolk Line. 111 was one of five Ransomes built vehicles with lowbridge bodies that entered service with the Lancashire town in the Spring of 1931. In front of the St Helens vehicle the turning circle for the Norwich Road Bridge short working was erected at the junction with Cromer Road. (S Lockwood collection)

44. Karrier 110 is seen in Norwich Road on route to Rushmere Heath and about to pass under the trailing junction of the Norwich Road Bridge short working turning circle. A short distance further on 110 will pass under the railway bridge seen in the previous view. An Austin A40 squeezes through the gap by the roadworks.
(H N James/Ipswich Transport Museum)

45. This scene depicts a post war vehicle negotiating the tight turning circle at Whitton next to The Maypole public house. Not an ideal location perhaps as the large notice requests "No Parking" and directs pub customers to an adjacent yard. The notice also points out the land is a "Tram Turning Circle"; many passengers continued to refer to trolleybuses as trams. Note the differing finials on the top of the standards in the turning circle. (C Carter)

From **Bramford Rd. Term.** to **Derby Rd. Station** (via. St. John's Road.)				
On Weekdays.			**On Sundays.**	
a.m.	p.m.	p.m.	a.m.	p.m.
7.10	12.0	6.0	10.13	4.20
7.20	12.10	6.10	10.23	4.30
7.30	12.20	6.20	10.33	4.40
7.40	12.30	6.30	10.43	4.50
7.50	12.40	6.40	10.53	5.0
8.0	12.50	6.50	11.3	5.10
8.10	1.0	7.0	11.13	5.20
8.20	1.10	7.10	11.23	5.30
8.30	1.20	7.20	11.33	5.40
8.40	1.30	7.30	11.43	5.50
8.50	1.40	7.40	11.53	6.0
9.0	1.50	7.50	p.m.	6.10
9.10	2.0	8.0	12.3	6.20
9.20	2.10	8.10	12.13	6.30
9.30	2.20	8.20	12.23	6.40
9.40	2.30	8.30	12.30	6.50
9.50	2.40	8.40	12.40	7.0
10.0	2.50	8.50	12.50	7.10
10.10	3.0	9.0	1.0	7.20
10.20	3.10	9.10	1.10	7.30
10.30	3.20	9.20	1.20	7.40
10.40	3.30	9.30	1.30	7.50
10.50	3.40	9.40	1.40	8.0
11.0	3.50	9.50	1.50	8.10
11.10	4.0	10.0	2.0	8.20
11.20	4.10	10.10	2.10	8.30
11.30	4.20	10.20	2.20	8.40
11.40	4.30	10.30†	2.30	8.50
11.50	4.50	10.40*	2.40	9.0
	4.40	10.50*	2.50	9.10
	5.0		3.0	9.20
	5.10		3.10	9.30
	5.20		3.20	9.40
† To Cornhill only	5.30		3.30	9.50
	5.40		3.40	10.0
	5.50		3.50	10.10
*To Barr. Cnr, only			4.0	10.20*
			4.10	10.30*
				10.40*

46.   Sunbeam 123 waits on stand prior to returning to town and then onwards to Rushmere Heath having completed the turn around the Whitton circle on the left. The differing finials can be seen again with the pointed version, a leftover from the tramway era, in the foreground and the later ball type design to the rear. A Fordson van can be seen leaving Whitton Church Lane. (C Carter)

Timetable 1926

BRAMFORD ROAD/ADAIR ROAD

47.   One of the three railway under bridges that the Ipswich trolleybuses had to contend with was on Bramford Road just beyond the Kingston Road short working terminus that carried the branch line for Felixstowe and the East Suffolk Line. The bridge is seen as originally built which was too low for trams and double deck trolleybuses. When the latter were introduced the route was extended under the bridge to Adair Road using single deck vehicles. In this view Ransomes 42 is about to pass under a section insulator/feeder before negotiating the bridge on its way to the Adair Road terminus in September 1953. (P Wilby/Ipswich Transport Museum)

48.   Ransomes 41 passes under the offending bridge on the last leg of the outward journey along Bramford Road to Adair Road. This was one of the original verandah style vehicles which is seen here after rebuilding. (A M Wright/Ipswich Transport Museum)

49.   The terraced houses on Bramford Road are the background to Ransomes 37 as it begins the turn into the Adair Road terminus. This vehicle was also from the batch that were originally dual entrance/exit with a verandah style front (see Picture 15) but were rebuilt as indicated with full front and closed off front entrance. (W J Haynes)

50.   Ransomes 42 waits at the Adair Road turning circle with The Waveney public house in the background. This batch of vehicles was also delivered as dual entrance/exit for one man operation but this was not successful due to slow loading times and as a result the front entrance was closed off. The advertising board surround mounted on the roof gave an awkward appearance; at least 50% of the space was not generating revenue when this view was taken in the late 1940s. Note the lining out on the body side panel and the trolleybus stop on the left.
(Ipswich Transport Museum)

ST MARGARETS STREET/ MAJORS CORNER

51.   This view looks like a scene from a Lancashire or Yorkshire mill town as Karrier 111 moves along St Margarets Street past the factory of Phillips & Piper, which is now converted into apartments. The overhead junction from Woodbridge Road can be seen in the background; just beyond this point behind the photographer's position was the Grey-Green coach depot that still carries the company name over the doorway.
(P Wilby/Ipswich Transport Museum)

52.   This view looks along St Margarets Street towards the junction with Woodbridge Road where the current Odeon cinema would be behind the advertising hoardings. Sunbeam 123 has just passed under the overhead junction onto parallel wiring on its way to St Augustines Church via Felixstowe Road. 123 will turn into Upper Orwell Street at Majors Corner whilst the nearside set of wiring leads into St Helens Street; the Woodbridge Road wiring (to the left of the advertising hoardings) had been removed by the date of this photograph in October 1961. Note the driver's overhead route indicator mounted on the left hand standard and the Tolly Cobbold lorry waiting to exit St Margarets Green. (J C Gillham)

53.   Karrier 113 moves along St Margarets Street just before reaching Majors Corner in September 1962; the site of the current Odeon cinema is to the immediate right. The nearside parallel wiring into St Helens Street has been removed in this view but the twin line hanger is still in place. (A Valentine)

⟶ 54.Ransomes 58 leaves Upper Orwell Street and negotiates Majors Corner around the standard in the middle of the road which, at the time the photograph was taken about 1950/51, formed a mini roundabout on which traffic lights were mounted. The now demolished Beehive public house is on the right and St Helens Street is to the left.
(D A Jones/London Trolleybus Preservation Society)

⟶ 55.This mid 1930s view depicts 49 from the first batch of Ransomes double deckers passing Majors Corner as it moves into St Helens Street on Route 5 to Foxhall Road closely followed by 5 the sole Tilling Stevens single decker. Light catches the burnished aluminium panels of the double decker as both vehicles pass under first generation overhead equipment. The wiring to the left at the top of the picture leads into Upper Orwell Street with the corner of The Beehive public house just in view on the extreme left. (Ipswich Transport Museum)

WOODBRIDGE ROAD/RUSHMERE ROAD/
COLCHESTER ROAD

56.   Pre-war Ransomes 83 leaves Woodbridge Road and enters St Margarets Street inward bound to Electric House. The destination display appears to have been set ready for the next duty to Foxhall Road whilst the policeman on point duty directs the traffic at a junction that is now controlled by traffic lights. (W J Haynes)

———→ A page from the British Insulated Callenders Cables (BICC) overhead equipment catalogue from February 1949, illustrated the junction from Woodbridge Road into Sidegate Lane on the left. Also included on the page are the components used in a typical turnout junction.

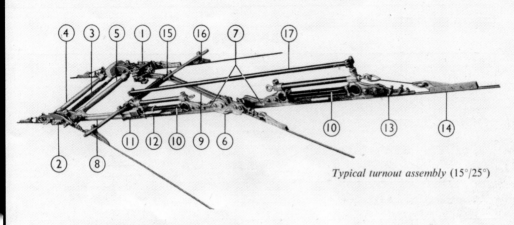

Typical turnout assembly (15°/25°)

REFERENCES

1 Leader frog, with hand or electrical operation

2 Companion frog

3 Insulated tie bar for tongue operation (turnouts only)

4 Wood spacer (long) : alternatively with single globe-and-link spacer

5 Wood spacer (short)

6 Crossing

7 Short runner (2 required)

8 Medium runner

9 Long runner (shown with reset device for hand-operated collector-reset or electrically-operated turnouts)

10 Insulator unit

11 Arc trap

12 Arc shield

13 Set-screw end fitting

14 Anchor ear, to reinforce trolley-wire connection

15 Insulated link connector (for 15°/25° arrangements)

16 Mechanical ear

17 Jumper

Electrically-operated Y turnout ; a lamp indicator box is mounted on the pole, together with emergency hand operating mechanism. A special feature is the use of curved runners with solidly-connected twin-line hangers to place the turnout some distance ahead of the branch road to prevent dislocation of traffic

←——— 57.Karrier 111, unusually in a very dirty condition, turns out of Sidegate Lane into Woodbridge Road on a peak hour return working to town. In this view the wiring into Sidegate Lane from the opposite direction, which can be seen in the BICC catalogue page, has been removed. Following 111 is a Hillman Minx saloon.
(H N James/Ipswich Transport Museum)

←——— 58.Karrier W 91 waits at the stop on the town side of Rushmere Road with the traffic island at the junction with Colchester Road in the background. The wiring to the right of the island continued along Colchester Road to rejoin Woodbridge Road East near Heath Road. There was provision for short working to the traffic island illustrated where the wiring can be seen to the rear of 91; the destination display for this duty was Colchester Road but with no route number allocated. (W J Haynes)

59.   This view illustrates the short working referred to above with Ransomes 86 passing under the overhead junction as it completes the move around the traffic island to reach the stand indicated in the previous view. The overhead wiring to the right of the junction continued along Colchester Road before joining Woodbridge Road East. The gateway to the rear of the Wolseley car is still in existence.
(S E Letts)

60. Leaving Woodbridge Road we travel the length of Sidegate Lane to the terminus just before the junction with Humber Doucy Lane. This route was one of the post-war extensions opening on 10th April 1947 and Karrier W 99 poses at the exit of the specially built turning circle before returning to Electric House. (A Valentine)

61. This view, taken in July 1949, depicts Karrier W 100 in Sidegate Lane having just left the turning circle and for some reason the conductor has had to use the bamboo retrieval pole. It is obviously a warm day as the driver has both the windscreen and side ventilator open. Note the "pre-fabs" in the background that are still a feature of the area having been built in 1946. (A D Packer)

ST HELENS STREET/SPRING ROAD/
RUSHMERE HEATH

62.   We are now looking along St Helens Street from Majors Corner in October 1961 with an unidentified trolleybus waiting to cross into Carr Street on its way to Whitton via Cornhill. A second trolleybus can be seen on the right leaving Upper Orwell Street to negotiate the overhead crossover into St Margarets Street and thence onward to Electric House. Note the Ford car in the foreground and the Gaumont cinema on the left (now the Regent Theatre).
(J C Gillham)

←———— 63. Sunbeam 123 leaves Spring Road and passes the Lattice Barn public house on the right as it moves into Woodbridge Road East on Route 3 to Rushmere Heath. This road junction was the original terminus before the extension to Rushmere Heath in April 1934 and was retained as a short working into post war years. 123 is about to pass under a line feeder/section insulator; the latter were required every half mile (0.8km). The milk delivery van on the right belongs to J Clark and the shop on the left is now a private residence. (C Carter)

←———— 64. A view in the opposite direction along Woodbridge Road East with Sunbeam 124 making its way to town on route to Whitton. A wide white band around the standard identifies the trolleybus stops on the corner of Goring Road and the opposite side of the road. Ipswich's second generation overhead wiring was a model of smooth running around bends and curves but the twin line hanger on the left immediately after the section insulator has quite a severe change in direction. (C Carter)

65. Karrier W 101 is seen at the Rushmere Heath terminus at the junction of Woodbridge Road East and Playford Road. The overhead wiring around the seated shelter has BICC 24" (610mm) spaced components that were fitted later than the wartime conversion of the majority of the system to second generation equipment. The shelter no longer exists. (C Carter)

66.   The "last of the summer wine" gentlemen sit in the shelter at Rushmere Heath whilst watching the photographer taking this view of Ransomes 41. It is one of the verandah front entrance pay as you enter vehicles delivered in 1929 and as mentioned earlier they were converted to full front with passengers using only the rear entrance/exit. Note the coat of arms on the verandah railings and the telegram advertisement, the latter being illuminated during the hours of darkness. (Ipswich Transport Museum)

FOXHALL ROAD

67.   A view taken on the last day of the Foxhall Road route on 31st May 1958 with an unidentified Sunbeam at the bottom of Grove Lane about to turn into St Helens Street. Note the standard supporting the overhead wiring positioned in the roadway of Warwick Road; this must have been a hazard for drivers during wartime blackout conditions.
(P Wilby/Ipswich Transport Museum)

68. Sunbeam 117 has just crossed Foxhall Road having negotiated the crossover after leaving Cauldwell Hall Road and entering Derby Road as it makes its way to Priory Heath and onwards to the Airport. The crossover was a special build from the earlier days of the system hence the 18" (457mm) spacing of the overhead as evidenced by the globe and link twin line hangers either side; hangers in the background are 24" (610mm) spacing using modern BICC components.
(H M James/Ipswich Transport Museum)

69. A rear view of pre-war Ransomes 61 in Foxhall Road pulling away from the stop at the bottom Wellesley Road as it makes it way forward towards the junction with Derby Road. The 18" (457mm) overhead spacing suggests a pre-war or immediate post war photograph with the 'D' shaped lower deck windows pointing to the latter.
(J Peach/Ipswich Transport Museum)

70.   Ransomes 83 swings around the traffic island that provided the terminus for the Foxhall
Road route and will complete the manoeuvre to reach the stand for the return to town. Wiring in
the foreground leads into Bixley Road and onwards to Felixstowe Road at St Augustines Church.
In the background the junction from Heath Road can be seen which led from Woodbridge Road
East. The circular routes '0' and specials used the wiring on these roads.
(S E Letts)

UPPER ORWELL STREET/FORE STREET

71.   Sunbeam 121 makes its way down Upper Orwell Street on Route 4 to St Augustines Church via Felixstowe Road with a second vehicle close behind. In the background is Majors Corner with Botwoods and the mini roundabout, in view. Note the narrowness of the street with the Rover taxi License Number 185 on the left in this August 1961 scene. (A D Packer)

→ 72.A little further down Upper Orwell Street Karrier W 107 is seen on the Gainsborough Estate circular in September 1962. Although a bracket arm has been used to carry the overhead wiring a curve has been introduced by the use of pull offs attached to the T bracket at the end of the arm. St Michaels Church is in the background and much of the property on the left of this street was being prepared for demolition at the time of writing. (A Valentine)

→ 73.Also in September 1962 Karrier 110 is seen en route to the Airport having crossed the Orwell Place/Eagle Street road junction and moving into the top of Fore Street. On the left is the long established ironmonger Martin & Newby where virtually any item of hardware could be obtained; the business closed in the summer of 2004. (A Valentine)

74.   Before the demolition of the Social Settlement buildings, which were on the immediate left, this junction was devoid of the traffic island which Sunbeams 115 and 120, seen leaving Fore Hamlet, are about to negotiate. The photographer is standing at the end of Fore Street and to the right is Duke Street leading to Holywells Road. The building with the clock is an electricity substation that fed the trolleybus system; it is now Mortimers Fish Restaurant. In the top left hand corner of the view is the automatic switch controlling the Fore Hamlet/Duke Street overhead junction. The picture dates from October 1961. (J C Gillham)

FORE HAMLET/FELIXSTOWE ROAD/
ST AUGUSTINES

75.   Snow still lays on the ground as Karrier W 107 leaves Fore Street and enters Fore Hamlet
in January 1963 as it passes Ipswich's Commer tower wagon PV 6283. The tower and crew's
accommodation were from an earlier tower wagon converted from a West Hartlepool Corporation
Bristol single deck bus. (A Valentine)

←————76.A busy scene looking along Felixstowe Road from the top of Bishops Hill in October 1961. Sunbeam 121 exits Nacton Road to drop down Bishops Hill on its way to Electric House whilst Karrier 111 enters Felixstowe Road on Route 4 to St Augustines. The female cyclist provides a perfect hand signal for a right turn into Nacton Road. (J C Gillham)

←———— 77.The use of the Ipswich system for testing Ransomes built trolleybuses has already been mentioned (see Picture 43) and here is a second example with a vehicle from the author's home town seen in what is thought to be Felixstowe Road. 101 was the only Ransomes trolleybus in the Derby Corporation fleet that was almost all of Guy manufacture prior to 1939. Ransomes also built the bodies for some of Derby's pre-war motorbuses. (University of Reading)

78.   The boy cyclist turns to make sure his friend is safe as Sunbeam 115 overtakes both them and the Bedford van on the return trip to town. The view dates from July 1962 and is near the junction of Felixstowe Road and Murray Road, the latter being to the right of the rear cyclist. Note the pre-war 18" (457mm) overhead spacing is still in use and the tramway style finial at the top of the standard on the left. (A Valentine)

79.   Two Garrett single deckers, 23 and 25 delivered in 1926, have passed in Felixstowe Road adjacent to the garage/filling station near King Edward Road. This pre-war scene is full of atmosphere with the garage signs, open tourer and white painted handcart in the foreground used to deliver milk and bread. (Ipswich Transport Museum)

80.   Karrier W 107 leaves the Felixstowe Road wiring to enter Cobham Road in July 1963; Kings Way is on the left from where the Mini is emerging. The Kings Way destination blind was somewhat confusing for anyone not familiar with Ipswich as the vehicle did not turn here and at this stage there was no wiring along this thoroughfare; it therefore indicated a Priory Heath depot working. The wide road junction seen above was the original terminus and subsequently Kings Way and Rands Way were wired to provide a connection between Felixstowe Road and Nacton Road. Later when Cobham Road and Lindbergh Road were wired to provide the same connection the Kings Way/Rands Way wiring fell into disuse but was retained unconnected for many years for electrical supply purposes. (H N James/Ipswich Transport Museum)

Timetable 1926.

From **King's Way** to **Cornhill** and **Bourne Bridge.**				
On Weekdays.			On Sundays.	
a.m.	p.m.	p.m.	a.m.	p.m.
6.47†	12.40SO	6.5	10.15	4.35
7.0	12.45	6.15	10.25	4.45
7.23	12.55	6.25	10.35	4.55
7.32	1.0 SO	6.26†	10.45	5.5
7.35	1.5	6.35	10.55	5.15
7.45	1.11†	6.45	11.5	5.25
7.55	1.15	6.55	11.15	5.35
8.5	1.25	7.55	11.25	5.45,
8.15	1.35	7.5	11.35	5.55
8.18†	1.40†	7.15	11.45	6.5
8.25	1.45	7.25	11.55	6.15
8.30†	1.55	7.35	p.m.	6.25
8.35	2.5	7.45	12.5	6.35
8.40†	2.15	7.55	12.15	6.45
8.45	2.25	8.5	12.25	6.55
8.55	2.35	8.15	12.35	7.5
9.5	2.45	8.25	12.45	7.15
9.15	2.55	8.35	12.55	7.25
9.25	3.5	8.45	1.5	7.35
9.35	3.15	8.55	1.15	7.45
9.45	3.25	9.5	1.25	7.55
9.55	3.35	9.15	1.35	8.5
10.5	3.45	9.25	1.45	8.15
10.15	3.55	9.35	1.55	8.25
10.25	4.5	9.45	2.5	8.35
10.35	4.15	9.55	2.15	8.45
10.45	4.25	10.5	2.25	8.55
10.55	4.35	10.15	2.35	9.5
p.m.	4.45	10.25†	2.45	9.15
11.5	4.55	10.35†	2.55	9.25
11.15	5.2	10.45†	3.5	9.35
11.25	5.5	10.52†	3.15	9.45
11.35	5.15		3.25	9.55
11.45	5.25	†To Cornhill only	3.35	10.5
11.55	5.35		3.45	10.15*
12.5	5.45		3.55	10.25*
12.15	5.46†	*To Barr. Crn.only	4.5	10.35*
12.25	5.55		4.15	10.41*
12.35			4.25	10.46*
		SO Saturday only		

81.   A view in the opposite direction looking towards the railway bridge over the line to Felixstowe; beyond the bridge is the St Augustines terminus and the top of the church tower projects above the skyline.   Karrier W 108 is about to join Felixstowe Road from Cobham Road with Kings Way on the extreme right.   Electrical feeders to the overhead can be seen at the top of the picture but without any insulated section breaker.   This road junction is now controlled by traffic lights.
(A D Packer)

82.   Sunbeam 117 turns round the traffic island at the St Augustines terminus with the named church in the background. The island and road junction still have kerbstones painted in wartime style black and white in this October 1961 view. The wiring from Bixley Road came in from the extreme left and the overhead junction taking wiring back to this road was immediately over the front of 117 where the splicing ears can be seen resulting from the removal of this fitting. (J C Gillham)

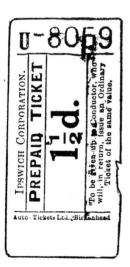

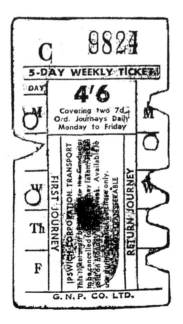

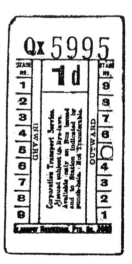

COBHAM ROAD/LINDBERGH ROAD

83.   Karrier 111 turns into Cobham Road off the Felixstowe Road railway bridge as it makes its way back to the Priory Heath depot; this was an extremely tight turn as indicated by the vehicle's position and the curve of the overhead wiring. The wiring leading out of Cobham Road and leaving the view to the left joined the town side of Felixstowe Road.
(H N James/Ipswich Transport Museum)

84.   This outward trip from the depot, which complements the previous view, has 111 travelling along a deserted Cobham Road towards Felixstowe Road on what is possibly a test run. The Priory Heath depot is in the background and is now the home of the Ipswich Transport Museum. The Museum has a number of tram, trolleybus and motorbus exhibits together with many other transport related items; a visit is highly recommended.
(H N James/Ipswich Transport Museum)

85.   This view, taken in the summer of 1963, depicts Karrier 114 parked in Cobham Road opposite the entrance to Priory Heath depot. The destination shows Kings Way and 114 has travelled the short distance from here to the depot entrance; passengers were allowed to travel to this point before vehicles entered the depot premises. The booms are just beyond the first set of overhead into the depot and to the rear is the exit wiring from Wright Road.
(H N James/Ipswich Transport Museum)

86.   Karrier 112 swings round the bend out of Lindbergh Road into Cobham Road in June 1963 as it returns to the depot a short distance further on. The conductor appears to have been having a chat with the driver as the internal bulkhead window is open. Note the location brackets for special slip destination boards below the nearside front windscreen and the advertisement for the local brew. Does any family recognise their pet? (J C Gillham)

87.   Smartly turned out Karrier W 106 hurries along the first stretch of Nacton Road on Route 6B to Gainsborough via Clapgate Lane. The junction at the top of Bishops Hill is in the background and Holywells Park is behind the wall on the left. Note the two differing styles of finials on the top of the standards in the foreground. (A Valentine)

← 88. Karrier 111 moves along Nacton Road at the junction with Clapgate Lane inward bound for Electric House in May 1962. The overhead Y junction for the two roads has solid runners to the first set of twin line hangers. The driver's indicator light showing which direction the overhead junction was set can be seen halfway up the supporting standard. A short distance along Nacton Road to the rear of 111 was the junction with Hatfield Road. (A D Packer)

← 89. A view in the opposite direction depicts Karrier W 108 leaving Clapgate Lane to join Nacton Road on its return trip to town on the Gainsborough circular having travelled outward via Duke Street and Holywells/Landseer Roads. Note the feeder cables to the overhead wiring adjacent to the central twin line hangers and the crossover. The view dates from June 1963. (J C Gillham)

90.   Sunbeam 116 is seen in Nacton Road on Route 2 to the Airport with Landseer Road wiring to the left and Rands Way on the right. Overhead wiring out of Landseer Road towards the town direction of Nacton Road can be seen; an earlier layout had wiring in the opposite direction but this had been removed by the time this view was taken in October 1961. Before the wiring of Nacton Road from here to Lindbergh Road vehicles turned into Rands Way to reach Kings Way and Felixstowe Road. (J C Gillham)

91.   The full circle of overhead wiring at the Nacton Road/Lindbergh Road junction can be seen in this October 1961 view of Sunbeam 115 making its way to the Airport. This rather heavy concentration of overhead featured in an immediate post war BICC trade catalogue. In the background is one of Ipswich's AEC Regent double deck motorbuses. (J C Gillham)

92.   Sunbeam 117 turns at the Airport terminus that was an extension along Nacton Road from Lindbergh Road opened on 17th August 1947. The Airport and terminal were to the rear of the photographer's position with the whole area now devoted to housing development other than the terminal buildings. To the rear of 117 are the factory premises of Crane Fluid Systems. (A Valentine)

Twin-Line Hangers

(U.K. Patent Nos. 424294 and 537899)

Four main types of twin-line hanger are shown below. All components are jig-assembled which ensures maximum interchangeability, facilitates repairs and replacement and reduces the stocking of parts to a minimum. Insulation is of porcelain or moulded composition, giving an adequate working margin even without the additional insulation provided by the span-wire insulators. Cast-metal parts are of special BICC non-corrodible lightweight alloy and steel components are all hot-galvanized.

The standard spacing for trolley wires is 24 inches but spacer bars of other lengths can be provided as required. Mechanical line ears can be fitted to suit any standard wire profile.

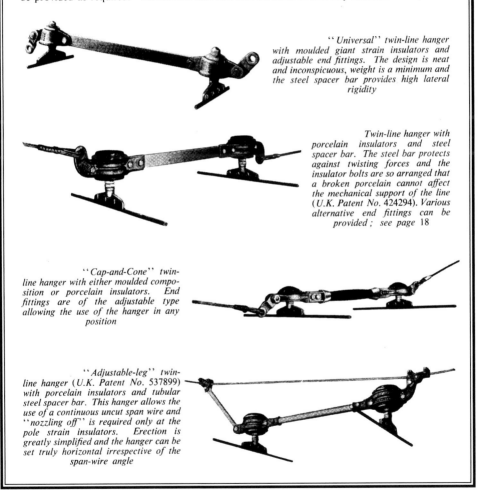

" Universal" twin-line hanger with moulded giant strain insulators and adjustable end fittings. The design is neat and inconspicuous, weight is a minimum and the steel spacer bar provides high lateral rigidity

Twin-line hanger with porcelain insulators and steel spacer bar. The steel bar protects against twisting forces and the insulator bolts are so arranged that a broken porcelain cannot affect the mechanical support of the line (U.K. Patent No. 424294). Various alternative end fittings can be provided ; see page 18

"Cap-and-Cone" twin-line hanger with either moulded composition or porcelain insulators. End fittings are of the adjustable type allowing the use of the hanger in any position

"Adjustable-leg" twin-line hanger (U.K. Patent No. 537899) with porcelain insulators and tubular steel spacer bar. This hanger allows the use of a continuous uncut span wire and "nozzling off" is required only at the pole strain insulators. Erection is greatly simplified and the hanger can be set truly horizontal irrespective of the span-wire angle

A catalogue page illustrating different types of twin line hangers. Ipswich's second generation fittings used the type shown in the second illustration but with straight span wire installations incorporating the adjustable leg attachments seen in the last illustration.

93.   The second railway crossing that had to be negotiated on the system was in Holywells Road and provided a connection between two Ransomes factory sites; Sunbeam 117 is about to cross the track on its way to Gainsborough in October 1962. To help with the location of this view the two bay factory building in the left background has been extensively refurbished and now houses a decorating centre. It had earlier been used by motor dealer Botwoods for commercial vehicles. (A Valentine)

94.   This August 1961 view depicts Karrier W 103 hurrying down the concrete surface of Landseer Road on a return trip to town from the Gainsborough Estate. The land to the right is now a major fuel distribution depot area and the Holbrook Road terminus, which existed before the 1940 extension along the road above, was at the top of the hill on the left. Note the 24" (610mm) overhead spacing that has been achieved by the use of 2:1 spacing links each side of the insulator. (C W Routh)

95.   The 1931 extension into the Gainsborough Estate, which terminated at Reynolds Road, was further extended along Landseer Road towards town in January 1938 to terminate at the junction with Holbrook Road. Karrier 110 drops down the hill on its way to Electric House with the wide entrance to Holbrook Road on the extreme right. (A D Packer)

D 2664345

DEC 61

P.V 8580

TOWER WAGON (WITH TRAILER)

AEC

2 months

29 E 60

96.   Karrier 111 is depicted in Landseer Road at the stop just before Clapgate Lane with the overhead junction for the latter immediately in front. The exit from Reynolds Road can be seen on the left beyond the second full width bracket arm; this was the last leg of the original "round the houses" terminus when the route into the Gainsborough Estate was first opened in July 1931. (A D Packer)

Sample ticket from the American issuing machine produced by Shanklin Rapid Transfer System, Springfield, Massachusetts and used on the first three experimental trolleybuses introduced in 1923.

97.　A view in the opposite direction with Karrier W 107 on stand before turning left into Clapgate Lane and thence back to the town centre. The wiring continuing around the curve of Landseer Road on the right joins Nacton Road opposite Rands Way (see Picture 90).　At one time the wiring from Clapgate Lane continued straight across the above junction exiting the view on the right to join the original one way "round the houses" terminus using Cotman and Reynolds Roads. Note the stop details painted on the pavement.
(A D Packer)

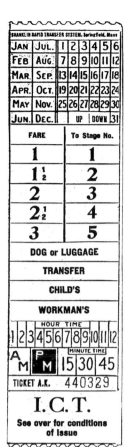

SHANKLIN RAPID TRANSFER SYSTEM, Springfield, Mass

JAN	JUL.	1	2	3	4	5	6
FEB	AUG.	7	8	9	10	11	12
MAR.	SEP.	13	14	15	16	17	18
APR.	OCT.	19	20	21	22	23	24
MAY	NOV.	25	26	27	28	29	30
JUN.	DEC.	UP		DOWN			31

FARE	To Stage No.
1	1
1½	2
2	3
2½	4
3	5
DOG or LUGGAGE	
TRANSFER	
CHILD'S	
WORKMAN'S	

HOUR TIME
| 1 | 2 | 3 | 4 | 5 | 6 | 7 | 8 | 9 | 10 | 11 | 12 |

A.M. P.M.

MINUTE TIME
| 15 | 30 | 45 |

TICKET A.K.　440329

I.C.T.

See over for conditions of Issue

Ipswich Corporation Tramways

Issued subject to Bye-Laws
and available on date of issue only to FARE POINT indicated by the number punched.

NOT TRANSFERABLE
To be retained on journey and given up before leaving car.

WORK PEOPLES' FARES
Tickets will be issued punched WORKMAN these to be retained & handed to the Conductor on entering Second Car for transfer journey, who will issue an ordinary ticket to cover the Transfer Journey.

Have your ticket ready to give up on completion of journey.

← ———— 98.Karrier W 102 stands in Reynolds Road on the original one way "round the houses" terminus for the Gainsborough Estate. This facility was removed in 1954 thus providing the final overhead layout for this area. (W J Haynes)

← ———— 99.Moving back along Clapgate Lane and the junction with Nacton Road, which can be seen in the background, Karrier 112 drives through the slush on a wintry day in January 1963 as it makes its way along the lane to Gainsborough. (A Valentine)

100. At the other end of Clapgate Lane Sunbeam 116 on the 6B Gainsborough circular makes a right turn, complete with semaphore direction indicator, into Landseer Road ready for the return to Electric House via Holywells Road in October 1961 (J C Gillham)

DEPOTS

101.   The Constantine Road (on the left) depot was built for the opening of the tramway system together with the power station (extreme left) and refuse destructor that is to the rear of the left hand bay. This view from October 1961 is taken from Portmans Walk (currently Sir Alf Ramsay Way) which continues along the right of the site. The depot was officially opened on 21st November 1903. The entrance for trolleybuses was from the rear with two wired access points and four additional roads inside requiring boom transfer. Previously there were two sets of wiring along Portmans Walk roughly from the second bracket arm that fed the depot access points. The exit wiring from the right hand bay previously joined that depicted just in front of the crossover. Exit wiring from the left hand bay was unconnected. The depot is still in use for the current Ipswich fleet. (J C Gillham)

102.   Priory Heath was opened as a depot and workshop in March 1937 and this October 1961 view shows the front of the site looking along Cobham Road towards Lindbergh Road. Access to the depot was via the two doorways and exit was at the rear via two similar doors with vehicles then proceeding along Wright Road to rejoin Cobham Road; this wiring can be seen on the right. Apart from the two through roads there were four others that required transfer of booms. The left hand bay included a paint shop and workshops. The depot was used by motorbuses for a while before closure and is now the refurbished site of the Ipswich Transport Museum.
(J C Gillham)

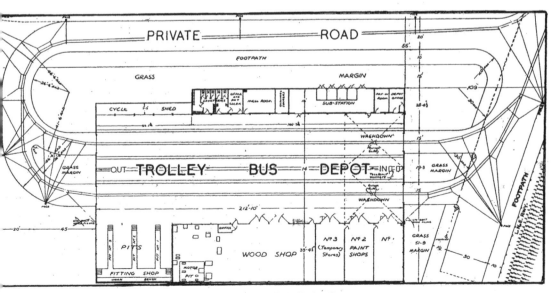

Layout of the New Ipswich Trolleybus Depot

ROLLING STOCK

103. **1923 1-3 Railless DX3970/88/06**

These were the first three vehicles, initially hired from Railless, for the pilot trolleybus scheme in Ipswich that was from Cornhill to the Station. Shorts of Rochester, Kent built the bodies with an open backed smoking area; 2 was enclosed by the Corporation in late 1931. Each vehicle seated 30 with 8 in the rear open compartment. They had two EEC 20HP motors and 1&3 were withdrawn late 1931/ early 1932 followed by 2 mid 1934. One of the batch is seen at the Station turning circle; note the "pay as you enter" sign on the forward step plus the stop/stage sign mounted on the standard. The notice in the window indicates a fare of 1d between Cornhill and the Station. 2 can be seen at the Ipswich Transport Museum.
(Tramway and Railway World/National Trolleybus Association)

104. **1924 4 Ransomes DX4648**

Purchased for the evaluation of a product from a local manufacturer prior to placing bulk orders this all Ransomes vehicle was fitted with a 35HP motor and single deck front entrance body

seating 30. Withdrawal came in 1934 after use for the Royal Show. 4 is seen undergoing demonstration in Princes Street whilst operating on trade plates. The view is of interest as the separate tram overhead wiring can be seen leading from Cornhill into Queen Street on the right. (Ipswich Transport Museum)

105. **1925 5 Tilling-Stevens DX5217**

Also possibly purchased for evaluation this vehicle lasted until 1934 after rebuilding. There is uncertainty in respect of the motor but the body was built by Ransomes with seating that is variously reported as 30 or 32 and with a front entrance. It is seen here after rebuilding on the north side of Cornhill with the exit from Lloyds Avenue immediately to the rear. (National Trolleybus Association collection)

106. **1926 6-20 Ransomes DX5622/5608-21**

Half the first bulk order for trolleybuses to replace the trams was placed with Ransomes who built the complete vehicles. Their 50 HP motors were fitted and the bodies were dual entrance/exit with seating reported as 30 when new. Front entrances were closed off in later years and pneumatic tyres fitted. Earliest withdrawals were in 1937 with nine lasting into post war years; 15/16 and 20 were the last to be withdrawn in June 1950 whilst 8 lasted until August 1951 as an overhead line lubricator. 9 is on display at the Ipswich Transport Museum together with the chassis of 16; also being worked upon is the chassis of 20. In this view 9 is seen not long after delivery at an unidentified location whilst on the then Route 5 to Foxhall Road. (Ipswich Transport Museum)

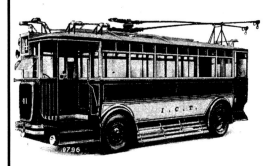

IPSWICH, ENGLAND.

Two types of Ransomes vehicles in the Ipswich electric trolley bus fleet.

First vehicle in continuous service since 1924.

15 ordered 1926.	1 ordered 1928.
5 ordered 1928.	3 ordered 1930.

Further extensions to the fleet are now in contemplation.

107.   1926 21-35 Garrett DX5626/23-25/28-29/27/30-32/34/33/35-37

The second half of the first bulk order was placed with another local manufacturer, namely Garrett of Leiston, and fitted with Strachan & Brown 30 seat dual entrance/exit bodies. Bull motors, probably 50HP, were fitted and the front entrance was closed off in later years. Earliest withdrawals were in 1937 with a few lasting into the immediate post war years. 25 is seen at the Station turning circle where additional bracket arms have been installed to support the overhead wiring (see Picture 103 for previous arrangement) and pneumatic tyres have been added (35 was the first trolleybus to be so fitted). 26 can be seen at the Ipswich Transport Museum and the chassis of 29, which was used as an overhead line lubricator from 1945-49, is on display in the Garrett Long Shop Museum, Leiston. (R Marshall)

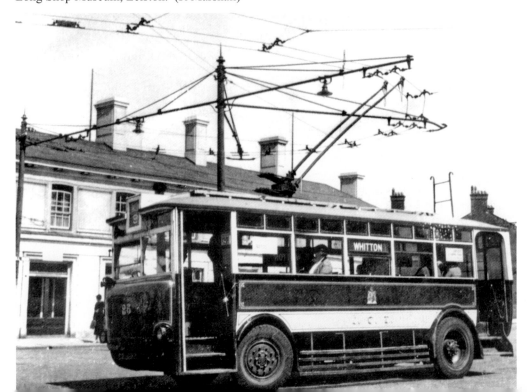

No picture. 1928 36 Ransomes DX6014

This was an all Ransomes demonstrator purchased by the Corporation and was fitted with a 34 seat dual entrance/exit body. It was similar in appearance to 6-20 but with an 8 bay construction (as opposed to 7) and fitted with red leather seats. It was withdrawn in 1940.

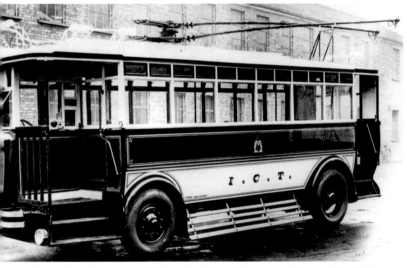

108. 1928/29 37-41 Ransomes DX7620/33/51/68/83

The next five vehicles were completely built by Ransomes but were unusual in having verendah platforms and half cabs to allow for front entrance one man operation with passengers exiting at the rear. Seating was for 30 when new and, with the exception of 41, all were new in 1928 with withdrawal taking place between 1950 and 1953. They were fitted with 50HP motors and the Corporation rebuilt the batch to full front design with front entrance (eventually closed off) and rear exit. (Author's collection)

109. 1930 42-44 Ransomes DX8869-71

These three vehicles were completely built by Ransomes using their 50HP motors and fitted with dual entrance/exit bodies with 31 seats; in later years the front entrance was closed off.

44 was presented to the then British Transport Collection in Clapham in 1955 and subsequently to the Science Museum in 1968; it is now in their storage facility at Wroughton near Swindon. The other two vehicles had been withdrawn in 1953. 44 is seen turning into Princes Street after leaving the Station forecourt. (W J Haynes)

No picture. **1931 45 Garrett DX9610**

This vehicle was originally intended as a demonstrator for continental markets but was purchased by Ipswich. It had a Bull 50HP motor and a central entrance body also by Garrett with seating capacity variously reported as 30 or 31. When delivered it was in red livery and was withdrawn in May 1937.

110. **1933 46-49 Ransomes PV 817-20**
1934 50-53 Ransomes PV1253-56
54-59 Ransomes PV1350-55   **1936 60-67 Ransomes PV2727-34**

1933 saw the delivery of Ipswich's first four double deck trolleybuses with the complete vehicles being built by Ransomes and with 46 being exhibited at the Commercial Motor Show; orders for a further 18 similar vehicles followed which were delivered in 1934/36. All were fitted with 80HP motors and 48 seat bodies but with a further 2 seats added during 1949/50. 46, 56 and 65 had their fronts restyled by the Corporation. First withdrawals were in 1948 (but not disposed of until 1950) and the last to go was 65 in April 1955. 46 is held by Ipswich Transport Museum pending restoration. In the view above 49 is caught outside the Cricketers Hotel. (C Carter)

111. **1937 68-73 Ransomes PV4061-66   74-79 Ransomes PV4540-45**
1938 80-85 Ransomes PV4788-93

The next three deliveries, whilst maintaining Ransomes chassis and motor (80HP) manufacture, were bodied by Massey Brothers based in Wigan, Lancashire. All were similar in appearance with 48 seat bodies when new which was increased to 54 seats in the period 1949-54. Earliest withdrawals were in 1954 with disposal the following year and the last departure was in 1959. 77 is seen on the Foxhall Road stand in Crown Street/Electric House. (C Carter)

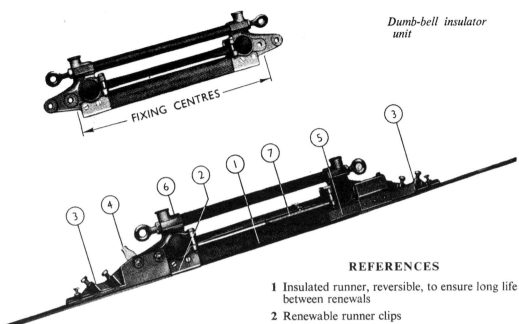

Dumb-bell insulator unit

FIXING CENTRES

Section insulator comprising insulator unit with trolley-wire end fittings

REFERENCES

1 Insulated runner, reversible, to ensure long life between renewals

2 Renewable runner clips

3 Trolley-wire end fittings of the set-screw type

4 Feeder cable socket

5 Arc trap at leading end

6 Boss suspension attachment (as feeder span) or for jumper connection (crossing)

7 Arc shield

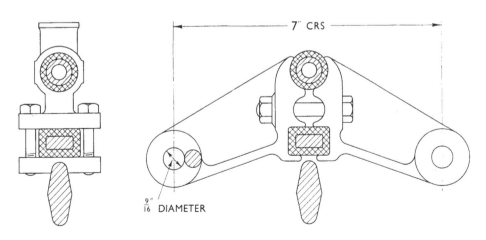

7″ CRS

$\frac{9}{16}$″ DIAMETER

(Left) *Section of insulator. The section of the insulated runner matches that of the standard trolley wire and ensures smooth, continuous profile run-through*
(Right) *Fitting for centre suspension*

(left)   112. **1940 86 Ransomes PV6426**

This was the last Ransomes trolleybus to enter service in the United Kingdom. There are suggestions that it was built as a demonstrator for a tour of the then South African market but no evidence can be found to support this view in either Ipswich's or Ransomes' records. It was fitted with a Ransomes 80HP motor and a 48 seat Massey body that was re-seated to accommodate 54 passengers in 1949. This unique vehicle was very popular with enthusiast photographers hence its numerous appearances in this volume. 86 was withdrawn in May 1958 and disposed of the following year. It is seen here at the Airport on an enthusiasts' tour. (A D Packer)

(lower left) 113. **1944 87-90 Karrier W PV6875-78**

These four vehicles were built to a wartime Ministry specified utility standard, hence the W reference in the chassis designation. They were fitted with EEC 80HP motors and rather severe angular Weymann bodies having 56 wooden slatted seats when delivered. The chassis were built at Sunbeam's Wolverhampton factory but "badge engineered" to carry the Karrier name, and entered service in the second half of 1944; they were withdrawn in the summer of 1958. 89 is seen waiting at the Foxhall Road stand in Crown Street/Electric House. (W J Haynes)

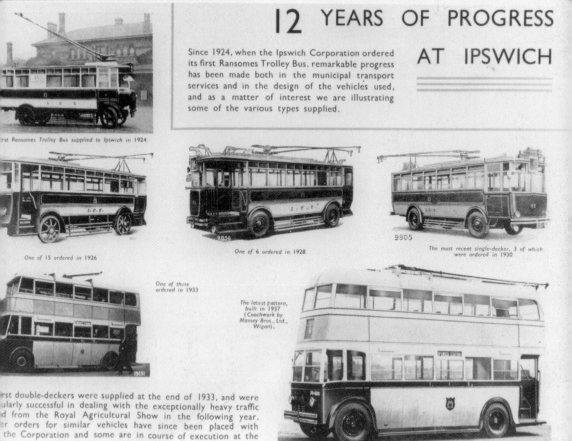

12 YEARS OF PROGRESS AT IPSWICH

Since 1924, when the Ipswich Corporation ordered its first Ransomes Trolley Bus, remarkable progress has been made both in the municipal transport services and in the design of the vehicles used, and as a matter of interest we are illustrating some of the various types supplied.

rst Ransomes Trolley Bus supplied to Ipswich in 1924

One of 15 ordered in 1926

One of 6 ordered in 1928

The most recent single-decker, 3 of which were ordered in 1930

One of those ordered in 1933

The latest pattern, built in 1937 (Coachwork by Massey Bros., Ltd., Wigan).

rst double-deckers were supplied at the end of 1933, and were ularly successful in dealing with the exceptionally heavy traffic d from the Royal Agricultural Show in the following year. er orders for similar vehicles have since been placed with the Corporation and some are in course of execution at the st time.

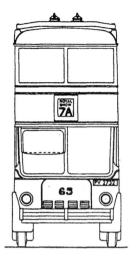
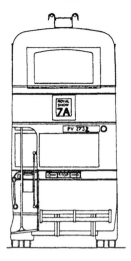

DRAWING No. TB6

IPSWICH CORPORATION
D/D. 4 Wheel. TROLLEYBUS.

TYPE:	SCALE:
RANSOMES 1934	4 mm = 1 foot.

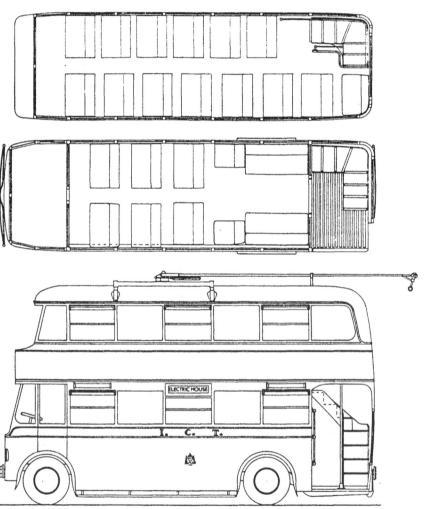

ELECTRIC HOUSE

I. C. T.

DRAWN BY:- TERRY RUSSELL, "CHACESIDE", ST.LEONARDS PARK, HORSHAM, W.SUSSEX. RH13 6EG.
SEND 4 FIRST CLASS STAMPS FOR COMPLETE LIST OF PUBLIC TRANSPORT DRAWINGS.

114. **1945 91-96**
Karrier W
PV6891-96
97-102 Karrier
W PV6950-55

91-96 were delivered in the first quarter of 1945 and the remainder in the period September to November. The chassis was again to the badge engineered W wartime Ministry specification and fitted with utility Park Royal 56 seat bodies. Motors were by Metro-Vick rated at 85HP with the first batch being withdrawn in March 1960 and the remainder during 1961. All were delivered in grey wartime livery with wooden slatted seats. 96 is caught under the overhead junction leading out of Heath Road into Woodbridge Road East. (W J Haynes)

115. **1948 103-108 Karrier W PV8268-73**   **1949 109-114 Karrier F4 PV8866-71**
1950 115-126 Sunbeam F4 ADX185-96

The last 24 vehicles were visually similar with the chassis all being built at Sunbeam's Wolverhampton factory and fitted with 56 seat Park Royal bodies. The first two batches carried the Karrier branding following the precedent set by wartime deliveries. All were powered with Metro-Vick electric motors; the Karriers were rated at 85HP and the Sunbeams 95HP. 119-126 from the last batch were sold for further service to Walsall in the first half of 1962 and when this Corporation's vehicles were absorbed into the West Midlands Passenger Transport Executive in 1969 all but one were transferred. All the Karriers were withdrawn between October 1961 and the closure of the system on 23rd August 1963; 114 was the last vehicle to operate. The remaining Sunbeams in Ipswich lasted until early 1963 and 126 (which was returned from Walsall) can be seen at the Ipswich Transport Museum together with 105 which is undergoing restoration. 120 is depicted outside the Cricketers Hotel. (C Carter)

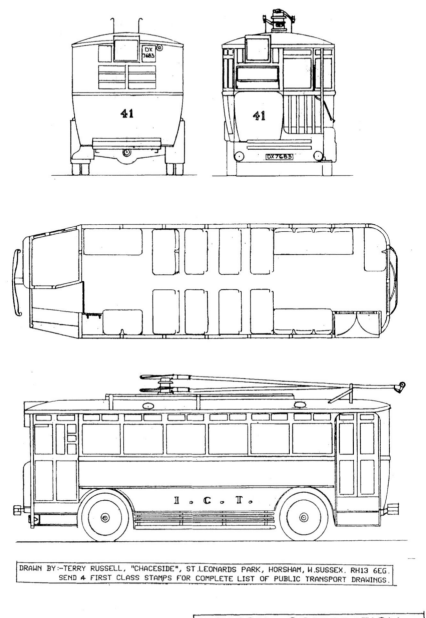

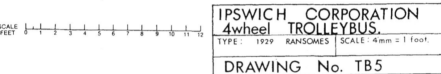

DRAWN BY:-TERRY RUSSELL, "CHACESIDE", ST.LEONARDS PARK, HORSHAM, W.SUSSEX. RH13 6EG.
SEND 4 FIRST CLASS STAMPS FOR COMPLETE LIST OF PUBLIC TRANSPORT DRAWINGS.

SCALE
FEET   0 1 2 3 4 5 6 7 8 9 10 11 12

IPSWICH CORPORATION
4wheel TROLLEYBUS.

TYPE: 1929 RANSOMES | SCALE: 4mm = 1 foot.

DRAWING No. TB5

TOWER WAGONS

116.   This view of the Ransomes battery electric tower wagon illustrates how the Electricity Supply and Transport Departments were operated as a single integrated unit as indicated by the wording on the front panel. However, by the time this photograph was taken in July 1949 the electricity supply industry had been nationalised and had passed out of the Corporation's control. Heavily involved with the overhead installation for the opening of the system in the 1920s this vehicle, complete with solid tyres, assisted with the removal of wiring after the closure in 1963. Note the two motors driving each of the front wheels. There were three other motorised tower wagons, namely an ex-West Hartlepool Corporation Bristol bus purchased in the early 1930s and converted into a tower wagon, an AEC Monarch (PV8580) and a pre-war Commer (PV6283) that can be seen in Picture 75. (J Meredith)

THE BEGINNING
AND THE END

117. The pilot trolleybus scheme commenced on 2nd September 1923 using three hired Railless single deckers. In this view 1 is seen outside the Station Hotel before completing the turn back into Princes Street and possibly positioned to show the manoeuvrability of the trolleybus compared to the tram. The pilot scheme was a success and led to one of the earliest UK tram to trolleybus conversions. (Tramway and Railway World/ National Trolleybus Association)

118. Almost 40 years later saw the end of the Ipswich trolleybus system on 23rd August 1963. Here 114, with a full load and suitably inscribed side panel, turns out of Nacton Road into Lindbergh Road on the final trip to Priory Heath depot. Thus ended virtually 60 years of electrically powered public transport on the streets of Ipswich provided by the trams and trolleybuses. (H N James/Ipswich Transport Museum)

THE AFTER LIFE

119.   As indicated in earlier text eight vehicles from the last batch of Sunbeam trolleybuses were sold to Walsall Corporation in 1962. Here Walsall 344 (Ipswich 123) has just passed under a section insulator/feeder in Wolverhampton Road, Bloxwich as it makes its way to the Mossley Estate. The vehicle passed to the West Midlands Passenger Transport Executive in 1969 and was withdrawn the following year. (W J Haynes/Ipswich Transport Museum)

120.   Walsall 351 (Ipswich 119) is seen at the rear of the ABC Cinema in Townsend Street, Walsall that was the loading point for Route 29 to Wolverhampton being jointly operated by the two municipalities. The all over blue livery of Walsall was in stark contrast to Ipswich's green, cream and burnished aluminium. The destination aperture provided a challenge for the blind maker, which was solved by printing "Wolverhampton" diagonally; even then it was a tight squeeze. The cinema site is now occupied by a large Woolworth store. 351 was also transferred to the West Midland Passenger Transport Executive and withdrawn in 1970. (Ipswich Transport Museum)

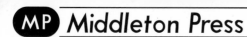

Middleton Press

Easebourne Lane, Midhurst, West Sussex.
GU29 9AZ   Tel:01730 813169

EVOLVING THE ULTIMATE RAIL ENCYCLOPEDIA

www.middletonpress.co.uk   email:info@middletonpress.co.uk
A-0 906520   B-1 873793   C-1 901706   D-1 904474

OOP Out of Print at time of printing - Please check current availability   **BROCHURE AVAILABLE SHOWING NEW TITLES**